# "GOOD MORNING! MORNING! HAVE A NICE DAY...."

By

# Elder Twila Lee Wynn

# KIRKUS
# REVIEWS

I N HER DEBUT RELIGIOUS TITLE, Wynn takes postings from her online presence and compiles a daily devotional.

Each selection begins with "Good Morning!" and ends with "Have a Nice Day..." These short snippets are designed to inspire and encourage readers, as are the biblical quotes sprinkled throughout the book. The book includes 124 daily devotions instead of the standard 365, and each devotional page has just one message on it. Some are shorter than others, but all are lighthearted and meant to convey a message about the comfort, support, love and mercy of Jesus Christ and God. As a licensed minister and ordained elder, Wynn attests that her warm smile—given freely to all she meets—radiates the warmth of Christ that lives in her heart. It's this warmth she puts in her work as she advises, "When you have accomplished your task at hand, and done the very best that you can do, you will receive your just reward!" (Day 16) Most readers will likely consider her words inspirational and comforting. However, not all of her advice is quite as sound: "When people who possess certain talents and skills come together to contribute to a project, there is no telling what they can do together. The Tower of Babel was the first proof of this." (Day 17) Some devotionals contain conflicting messages, and the content of others can be so short that it feels incomplete, as with Day 6: "You were chosen even before you were born, that is how special you are and your purpose."

A heartwarming, inspirational read.

# Foreword

## By Rev. Josephine Thompson

FIRST, I WANT TO THANK Elder Twila Wynn for having confidence in God to embrace the endeavor of writing this book. Secondly, I want to thank Elder Twila, my friend, for choosing me to write this forward. Thanking God for our relationship that has developed over breakfasts at Eat N Park. I discovered the secret of the "smile on her face" is nothing more than the Love of God shining through her to touch the lives of all she encounters.

Elder Twila Wynn has been called by God to share daily words of inspiration to the Facebook Family. Little did she know when she began to write out of obedience where the Lord would take her. Daily she sought God for a fresh word and new revelations to minister to others. Now, God has blessed her with this book, *"Good Morning! Have a Nice Day...."* which is a ministry tool that can reach others outside the Facebook realm. If you want your daily walk with the Lord to be strengthened, I encourage you to read this book from front to back, take notes, and keep it close to you for continual strength. This book is full of inspiration which you can immediately apply to your life.

*"Good Morning! Have a Nice Day...."* is filled with practical and applicable biblical scriptures and principles. It will encourage you to get in position to live out your God given purpose. So be blessed and inspired as you read this book.

# Dedications
# and
# Special Acknowledgments

T HIS BOOK IS DEDICATED to God who gave me the vision to write. God said, "This will be the first of many books." So I began to write out of obedience and the book is the fruit of the work.

I would also like to dedicate this book to my mother, Mrs. Olivia Vaughn Wynn, who taught me from an infant to love and worship God and about HIS son Jesus Christ. My mother passed away when she was forty-eight years old, and I was six. She had me in the house of God from the very beginning of my life, until the day the LORD called her home. My mother Olivia, read the word of God to me daily, and taught me how to pray, if it had not been for the Lord on her side, I don't know where I would be today. Thank You my most HOLY FATHER, for choosing Olivia Vaughn Smith-Wynn to be my mother.

I also have to give credit to my foster mother, Mrs. Ida Mae Alsop, whom I have called Aunt Ida Mae from the first day I met her and she welcomed me into her home, June 24th, 1974. We have been together for thirty-seven years. Aunt Ida is also a mighty woman of God; she is ninety-seven years old at this writing. God has kept her as she lives still alone, on her own, loving and worshiping the King of Kings, and His son, Jesus Christ, by the power of His Holy Spirit. Aunt Ida took the reins from where my mother Olivia left off, mind you, she had a whole lot to remold, but God our Father gave her His Strength to put me back on the right track. I want to thank you most Holy God for choosing Aunt Ida to be my foster mother.

The next person I want to acknowledge is Mrs. Jacquelyn Minor, who recently passed away. Mrs. Minor was the mother of the church where I attend. I would go to her home and spend many afternoons with her, where she poured her godly wisdom into me, and listened to me share about my past, and help me to understand why and how people do the things they do when they don't have a true relationship with Jesus. Once, when I was experiencing some very difficult situations, Mother Minor turned to me and told me to hold on, even if I had to hold on by my fingernails. She left me a letter when she went to be with the Lord. Her advice to me was "walk in Holiness for without it no one shall see the Lord, to be humble, to be forgiving, and to follow the teachings of Christ on the Sermon on the Mount." The great commission was the calling of the disciples.

## *Honorable Mention*

THIS IS FOR MY THREE CHILDREN, Jonathan Lindale Wynn, Susan Jo Saavedra, and Michael Edward Wright; and most of all, for my ten grandchildren and the one on its way: Alexandria, Tigris, Skye, Jonatha, Johnathan, Sara, Ania, and Tearo Wynn; my eldest grandson Jeffrey A. Jenkins II and my youngest grandson, Joaquin E. Saavedra IV. I love you all! I want you all to know that with God all things are possible, that is why I wrote this book. We all must learn to stand in the strength of the Lord, and the power of His might, but most of all His wisdom. My life has not always been easy, but I want you to know that it has always been favored by God, for when there is something for you to do for others; you will experience difficulties, so that you can see how His hands and wisdom has brought you out. What the Lord has done for me, He will do for you, as long as you trust and walk with Him, and live with Jesus Christ as the head of your life.

To my sister in Christ and friend, Rev. Josephine Thompson, who would share long, and I do mean very long, breakfasts with me at Eat N Park. The Lord led me to ask her to do the forward for HIS project; *"GOOD MORNING! HAVE A NICE DAY...."* You can only ask someone to this task that shares the same heart of Christ with you and loves you with the heart of Jesus. Thank you Pastor Josie, I love you.

To my dear sister, Emma Jean Jackson-Harris; let me take the time to make you all laugh. I am not computer savvy; however, Emma is. Remember, I said that the Lord led me to write in Facebook. Well, I didn't know that I should have been transferring my daily post into a Word document. I had been writing, or should I say typing for well over a year. I lost a majority of that content. My sister helped me to retrieve sixty days of writing, which you will now enjoy. She was also kind enough to edit this book as well. Thank you Emma, and I want to also thank Lori Lizik who did the proofing for the book proof for me, thank you both.

There are a host of others that I want to thank for their contributions to this project: to Jamye Sucecic for your encouragements and your belief in my dreams and goals; and, to Tim Fuge, my co-worker, for your computer advice; and Zen Chiang for the suggestion for the color of the cover, thanks to you both. I want thank Elder Milton and Elder Linda Dean, and Linda, who told me, the Lord said, "the book is not done until it's on the market;" may God bless you both. Last, but not least, my cover design man: I want to thank Mr. Jeffrey Green, of Green Studios, Farmington, PA. He so graciously offered his talent and skill for the cover of *"GOOD MORNING! HAVE A NICE DAY...."*

# Preface

THIS IS AN INTERACTIVE READING and writing book. Read the inspirational passages and write down your thoughts, see what is really inside you. Be willing to let God renew you minds and hearts through applying His Holy Principles.

How I was led to write this book by the Lord was, one day upon awaking, the Lord said, "write", this is your first book. He led me to Facebook. I began with Good Morning Face book, and I wrote my first post. I found that you could only use 430 characters at each post, which was good, but I had to shorten my openings to, Good Morning, and I would end my inspirational post with, Have a nice day.

What is very important to me is to share with you that this is not another New Age Book that will tell you that just by thinking positive, all is well, and that you have all this goodness inside of you. No, this book is inspired by the Holy Scriptures. We all have, families, and jobs, we are single, and we are married, we are men and women, but we are nothing without GOD, the one and only, King of Kings, and His Son Jesus the Christ, and empowered by His HOLY SPIRIT. I would not have been capable to this project with out all three. Thank you, God, thank you Jesus, thank you HOLY SPIRIT.

I've had some difficult paths to walk to be where I am today, but no matter what, the LORD kept me. The wisdom of GOD, has allowed me to speak and to smile at others just to let you know what He has done for me, He will do for you. The days when we all need to be uplifted, both men and women, we will be encouraged each day. There is no set pattern to the writings, so that what ever you will read, it will trigger something inside you to make you smile, and think. Then write a note to yourself that will make your thoughts stick! Enjoy.

# Introduction

THIS BOOK IS TO EMPOWER, embolden, and to edify you, for daily living, all we can do for one another is to be there with an open ear, and words of encouragement now and always. Good Morning! Have a Nice day.... will change your life. I pray this will help you as much as it has helped me in writing it, because I need to be encouraged as well. My hope is that by reading the inspirations in this book that it will warm your heart like a hot cup of coffee or tea will warm your soul. Enjoy, Have a nice day....

## 1 Thessalonians 5:11-18 CEV

[11] That's why you must ENCOURAGE and help each other, just as you are already doing.
[12] My friends, we ask you to be thoughtful of your leaders who work hard and tell you how to live for the Lord. [13] Show them great respect and love because of their work. Try to get along with each other. [14] My friends we beg you to warn anyone

who isn't living right. Encourage anyone who feels left out, help all who are weak, and be patience with everyone. [15] Don't be hateful to people just because they are hateful to you. Rather be good to each other and everyone else.

[16] Always be joyful [17] and never stop praying. [18] Whatever happens, keep thanking God because of Jesus Christ. This is what God wants you to do.

# Day 1

Good Morning! May the glory of God over take you today with favor as you go about His business of spreading joy to others, even in difficult situations. You are the light of the world, like a city on a hilltop that cannot be hidden, read Matthew 5:14. Have a nice day....

# Day 2

Good Morning! A friend of mine told me how she will randomly buy lunch for the person who's in line behind her at work, and another person told how they have bought gas for someone else when they were getting gas. These random acts of kindness are called paying it forward, and it pleases the Lord. The Lord also tells us not to cast our pearls before swine, which means some people will not appreciate your wisdom or kindness, but you keep doing what is right before the Lord, and it will come back to you at a later time. I challenge you to do something unexpectedly kind for someone else today and let's make a difference. Have a nice day....

# Day 3

Good Morning! Starting your day with a great breakfast is essential to having good energy for your day. Sending out healthy encouragement is essential to you knowing someone is wishing you well in your endeavors for the day. Have a great day everybody and know you are loved. Have a nice day....

# *Day 4*

Good Morning! Peaceful sleep has prepared you for a fit day. Sending hugs; for the arms of our Lord abounds around you for your protection. No weapons formed against you shall prosper. Have a nice day....

# Day 5

Good Morning! Do you know that no matter what you do in this life as your job, you have another gift that was given to you by your Father in heaven to use for others. Use it well so that you and others may be blessed. Mine is the gift of hospitality and encouragement. Whatever yours is, use it well. Have a nice day....

# *Day 6*

Good Morning! You were chosen even before you were born, that is how special you are and your purpose. Have a nice day....

# Day 7

Good Morning! Love… do we really love others? Please pray for those that do not know Christ yet. Those are the very ones He came for, just as He came for you and me before we came to know Him. People only act the way they do because their minds have not been renewed by Christ. Love them and pray for them. Have a nice day....

# *Day 8*

Good Morning! To all the beautiful friends and families out there in Facebook land, enjoy your weekend and all the blessing from above, for every good and perfect gift comes from God! God bless you all! Have a nice day....

# Day 9

Good Morning! When you go to church today, remember there are going to be people around you that will need to see you live out what you heard. Let us make our FATHER look good by the way we live. Know you are not alone, because Christ is with you for He will never leave you alone. Have a nice day....

# *Day 10*

Good Morning! The beginning of a brand new week; go in the willingness of knowing that every good and perfect gift comes from God. He will use anyone; even your enemies. He wants to bless you. We must be in the will of God to receive all of his many blessings. Know that you are loved and appreciated. Have a nice day....

# Day 11

Good Morning! Try your best to agree with one another. Do not take sides. Always agree with what you know is right, this is good for the soul and the body. It does not do you any good to have strife inside your soul for an unjust cause. Have a nice day....

# *Day 12*

Good Morning! Beautiful are the feet of those that carry the good news of the gospel. Read all Romans 10. Remember you are the carrier of something good for someone else today, to make them smile and uplift their spirit. Go forth with joy, someone is waiting. Think more of others than yourself and all will be well. Have a nice day....

# Day 13

Good Morning! There is a heat wave about to come I am told. Let us not complain; we could have 6 feet of snow, howling winds, and sub-degree temperatures; so let us be content in all things and get to a pool. This will not be as hot as hell where there is no relief. Have a nice day....

# *Day 14*

Good Morning! Because thine heart was tender, and thou did humble yourself before God, when you heard his word against this place and the people, and humble yourself before me, and tore your clothes, I have heard you. Read 2 Chronicles 34: 27-28. Pray for our country. I love you and God and Christ loves you more! Have a nice day....

# *Day 15*

Good Morning! When you give a gift to a friend, and you give it from your heart, do it for God's glory and not to be seen of men. When the woman who gave two mites, gave from her heart it was more acceptable to the Lord than those who gave hundreds and thousands. Remember God looks at the heart! Have a nice day....

# *Day 16*

Good Morning! When you have accomplished your task at hand, and done the very best that you can do, you will receive your just reward! All is well, all is well! No one can stop the law of completion. The thing to remember is for you to know that you are done, so you can move onto the next thing. Have a nice day....

# *Day 17*

Good Morning! The way that most tasks are accomplished is by teamwork. When people who possess certain talents and skills come together to contribute to a project, there is no telling what they can do together. The Tower of Babel was the first proof of this. When we come together, we all learn just how much we need and depend on one another. I need you just as much as you need me, and we both need someone else. (No man is an island, quote by John Donne). Not one of us was meant to stand alone. Have a nice day....

# *Day 18*

Good Morning! For every question that you will have, there is a correct answer. The knowledge of God must come with understanding; we are not to lean to our own understanding. When you need an answer open the bible, go to the back, look up the subject, and search the matter out. Have a nice day....

# Day 19

Good Morning! What a wonder our Lord is. His mercies are new each and everyday, He has great things planned for you today. Yesterday is gone, tomorrow is not here, so let us enjoy the present of today. I love you, but God loves you even more, that's why He sent Christ, and gave you His Holy Spirit. Have a nice day....

# Day 20

Good Morning! I have a dear friend that I see almost every day. She never fails to tell me that she loves seeing my smile, and it makes her happy when I come around. My friend always tells me that there is such a light around me and how much others love being around me, (they must have these conversations among themselves). I love my friend and I thank her for the compliments, but; I always share with her the same thing, it's not me, but the love of Christ coming through me, and I thank her for seeing Him in me. She tells me that I have to take credit too, because it's the choices that I make daily to let that happen. You see, the reason why I'm sharing this is; because, I know without Christ I am nothing, and can be nothing worth while, so I give our Lord all the credit for the changes that He has made in me, and you should too. Let us always give credit to our Holy Re-Creator who made us anew. Have a nice day....

# Day 21

Good Morning! Remember, with God all things are possible, to those who believe and live in obedience. He is a rewarder of those who seek His face first; for when you seek His face first, all other things will follow. God is in the smallest details of our lives, for He and Jesus loves you so. Have a nice day....

# *Day 22*

Good Morning! Laughter does the body good and is good for the soul. Think of something you did or something that someone said that will make you laugh. What a great way to change your atmosphere. I make myself laugh often and keep a smile on my face. Let's be like Timothy and don't forget to cheer ourselves up. Have a nice day....

# *Day 23*

Good Morning! Do you know all the benefits and promises that belong to you? When you get an insurance policy, you read it to know what you get when you are in trouble. Well, that is what you do with the bible, you have all that is in it, but how can you claim your benefits if you don't read the policy, the bible. Have a nice day....

# Day 24

Good Morning! Will you be willing to talk of Christ, of His love and strength to someone whom you may meet today? They may need to hear of Him and be encouraged. Have a nice day....

# Day 25

Good Morning! Pray for our country. We have turn away from the ways of the Lord. God our King will hear the prayers of the righteous. Pray that His will, will help us with the debt ceiling. If you have a credit card and can't pay your bill, why would you want a higher limit? Would you not trim your budget so that you can first pay what you owe? Have a nice day....

# *Day 26*

Good Morning! Know the truth of what God says about you. It's all good! Have a nice day....

# Day 27

Good Morning! Did you know that if someone you work for is not paying you fairly and withholding your due wages; that those wages are crying out to God, and our God hears those shouts along with your cries of unfairness. Read James 5:1-6. Have a nice day....

# $Day$ 28

Good Morning! Whatever you do today, do it with all your heart and unto the glory of God! Have a nice day....

# Day 29

Good Morning! The cross is more than mere jewelry. It is the sign of Gods love for us. It was the sign in the desert as to the way the tribes of Israel were assembled in the desert, with the cloud of God in the center. The cross is the sign of love and sacrifice. To know what love is, read Matthew 5:43-47. Have a nice day....

# $\mathcal{D}ay$ 30

Good Morning! Friendship... How important is it to you?
It is easy to be friendly to those you associate with, but what
about those that are not in your circles? Do you go out of
your way for those others? Christ went out of his way for
us, (Gentiles), to include us in his body, and that is what we
should do for others. Who did you tell about Christ lately?
Have a nice day....

# *Day 31*

Good Morning! Believe in the prayers that you put before the Lord. All that you've asked for in faith will come to pass according to his precious plan. Rejoice right now, thank Him right now. Sometimes sooner, sometimes later, but the prayers of the righteous will prevail. Have a nice day....

# Day 32

Good Morning! What will hell offer you here on earth that will make you turn your back on God and what you know is right, for the pleasure that will last for only a little time? The Lord said, "After sin has brought you pleasure; it will then bring you death." Friends think! Have a nice day....

# Day 33

Good Morning! I am reminded of the story of two sons. The one said he will go into the field and work and went not, and the other said, he will not go, but he eventually went. Which one are you? The one son looked like he was doing the right thing, but the one who was blessed is the one who did the right thing, Read all Matt 21. Have a nice day....

# Day 34

Good Morning! Follow your higher calling. Give to others when you have little. If there is something that you need in your life, help others with the little you have. An open hand will cause God and others to plant in your life. Give freely from your heart and watch doors open. Have a nice day....

# Day 35

Good Morning! God is so good! When I think of all the little things that He has done for us; the things that He does for us when we least expect it, it just makes me want to say, thank you Lord. Someone just gave me flowers for being nice. Is it that I'm so nice or just that others don't take time to be considerate of others? Be kind to someone today as you go about doing your job, you might be the only way someone sees Christ. Have a nice day....

# *Day 36*

Good Morning! Be nice today, because some people take pride in not being nice. Say I'm sorry to someone when you slip. It is easy, just remember everything you where taught in kindergarten. Keep it simple and smile. Have a nice day....

# Day 37

Good Morning! Don't be afraid to take that first step into greatness. Greatness is doing something with the passion that God gave you that will open doors and inspire others. Whatever it is that you do, do it with zeal unto the Lord! Have a nice day....

# *Day* 38

Good Morning! You are empowered for others. All that
you have gone through was to make you stronger, so you
can lead the way. How can you gain true wisdom of a situation without trials? God has given you the true gift of
experience, so share the patience of that experience, so that
Christ will be glorified. Have a nice day....

# Day 39

Good Morning! Put your faith to work, and do what God gave you to do. Someone is waiting on your gift to be a help to them. If you don't know how to get started.....ask the Lord, and be led by the spirit. Most of the things that God gave you to do is bigger than you anyway, that's why He tells us we can do all things through Christ who strengthens you. Have a nice day....

# Day 40

Good Morning! What is in a name? A rose by any other name is still a rose, (quote by Shakespeare, from play Romeo & Juliet), right. Well, the name of Jesus, the Lord, is the name above all names. So, call His name this morning with meaning and purpose and see His blessings come your way. Cry out to Him in worship, for His desires toward you are very pleasant, open the door and let him in. Have a nice day....

# Day 41

Good Morning! Do you know when you are led by the spirit of God, you can only do what He allows you to do and go where He wants you to go. When you live this way, there will be no excuses as to why you are not in the right place doing exactly what you are called to do. Read Acts 16:6-10. Have a nice day....

# Day 42

Good Morning! Do as God does. After all, are you his dear child. You are God's people, so don't let it be said that any of you are immoral or indecent or greedy. Don't use dirty or foolish or filthy words. Instead say how thankful you are. Read Ephesians 5:1-4. Have a nice day....

# Day 43

Good Morning! This one is funny. Last night I had a dream that I had bright green braids. I asked, "What is this?" The Lord said, "I love you just the way you are." Point is: God made us all different, no two are alike and we are all special to God. Come to him with all your flaws and He will change them for your good and His glory! I was glad when I woke up and my hair was normal... LOL. Have a nice day....

# *Day 44*

Good Morning! How you start this day will affect others, a smile, and a nod of your head of acknowledgement. If something is broken in your life, it will be impossible to help others. Come and let God be a repairer of any breach that is broken in your life so that you can move forward to do his will for others. Have a nice day....

# Day 45

Good Morning! Are you the one that leads the way; that leads others out of darkness? Are you the one that the light of the Lord is shining through? Are others happy to see you when you walk into the room? Are you the one that people bring others to when they need to be encouraged? If so, you are my true family in Christ and God is so proud of you and loves you and so do I. Have a nice day....

# Day 46

Good Morning! The soul that sins shall die. Adam didn't believe this when he was told; Satan made him doubt his creator. He didn't die physically, but his soul did. He was separated from God as soon as he was disobedient. We have Jesus who will save all who comes to Him. Stop listening to the wrong voices. Stop living ungodly. Have a nice day....

# Day 47

Good Morning! Starting a new season should create such a high hope in us that will bring about much rejoicing. There is a hope that Christ has given us all to keep us moving on and upward. Remember your gifts will make room for you. What God has called forth shall be used for his entire kingdom. I speak full release in Jesus name. Have a nice day....

# Day 48

Good Morning! What is life without respect? What is worth it in life without integrity? You can't say you have respect for a person in your heart and then disrespect them with your actions. Only God knows the heart of a man, but we see what you really think by the way you live. Let God and Christ create a new heart in you, so that everything lines up righteously with Christ's character. Have a nice day....

# Day 49

Good Morning! Time is short, get ready, Christ is coming back soon! Think and make changes in your life before it is too late! Have a nice day....

# Day 50

Good Morning! Do you really know how much love you have inside of you for others; the same amount that God had for you that He sent His son, the Christ, to show you? Please give and share it just to make God and others happy. Life is so short, just a vapor, a mist. Please don't withhold the gift. Holy Spirit is the power that lives inside of you to enable you to give it. Have a nice day....

# *Day 51*

Good Morning! Remember, there are two worlds; spiritual and the natural. When you are going through a thing, remember, if you are walking with Christ, all is well. We must stay focused on the coming out, this is only temporary. Don't let the situation seem bigger than the God you serve. The trials are what build your character. Remember, no weapons formed against you shall prosper, Read Isaiah 54. Have a nice day....

# Day 52

Good Morning! There is the athlete, the farmer, and solider, what do all three have in common? They press on until the end: The athlete onto the finish line, the farmer until the harvest, and the solider until the war has been won. There is a space of time before we receive what we seek from the Lord. Please don't give up until you have what you have trusted him for. He that endures to the end shall receive his reward, Read 2 Timothy 2.

# Day 53

Good Morning! Simply Good Morning! Enjoy your day. Sometimes we just need to reflect that we have a new day; that the Lord has kept us and our family safe through the night. This leads you to a higher hope of resting in him. Have a nice  day....

# Day 54

Good Morning! This is the beginning of a new school year and some are off to college. We are all going to school; it's called the school of life. Some will learn and apply righteous principles of the Lord; others will just exist in the classroom of life and won't receive the benefits offered to all by Christ. We are called to a higher standard of learning to benefit others in the kingdom of God. Have a nice day....

# Day 55

Good Morning! Love is so powerful it is a force to be reckoned with; it will cause you to pray for your enemies and cry out to God for those that you see that are lost. There is so much evil in this world around us; we can't deny; the evil we see are evil spirits using a person. When it is finished in them, it will leave them crippled and lame. Please use your power of love to pray for them and not to complain about them. Prayer changes things. Have a nice day....

# Day 56

Good Morning! Dreams are giving by the almighty God. They spring up from a well deep inside of us. Dreams lead to accomplishing things that we might never have thought possible: look at the Wright Brothers; Mark Twain; and George Washington Carver; Dr. Martin Luther King and what they achieved. What will your dreams bring forth to honor God and others. Dream big! Have a nice day....

# *Day* 57

Good Morning! I'm so glad that God gave me a voice. It can be used to tell others; you can make it. I'm so glad God gave me a voice to tell you; don't give up. I'm so glad God gave me a voice to say; too late. I'm so glad God gave you a voice. How will you use it to uplift yourself and others today? Paul tells Timothy to cheer others up when you instruct them, and always be patient, 2 Timothy 2. Have a nice day....

# *Day 58*

Good Morning! When Jesus spit in the ground and made mud that healed the blind man's eyes. He then told him to go and wash in the pool of Siloam (which means one who is sent); when he washed off the mud he could see. Read John 9. When someone comes to bless you, don't look a gift horse in the mouth, be thankful. If you are the one that is blessing someone, do the deed and move on just as Jesus did so that the entire honor goes to God. Have a nice day....

# Day 59

Good Morning! I witnessed something so wonderful yesterday. A friend came to me to see if I remembered what her friend liked the day before when I was assisting them both. I didn't truly remember and said so. This lady wanted to surprise her friend with a gift, while she was deciding; the other friend came by and asked what she was up to. The friend said she wanted to surprise her, so she asked point blank which one she liked. When her friend told her, she was glad, and the other friend said they could share the item, but she herself was going to pay for it. The friend then told me that she was going to surprise her friend with the gift that she wanted to first give to her, and it was going to be a true surprise. This was the president of a top organization and one of her top leaders. This lesson is what I try to convey to others daily. Give with your whole heart, and it will be given back to you. You can always get by with a little help from a friend. Have a nice day....

# Day 60

Good Morning! About 4 years ago while I was on my way to work, I was singing to the Lord, (He said to make a joyful noise to him), I was singing, I love you Lord, I bless you Lord, repeating this over and over. The Lord said to me, "Feed my sheep." I stopped, and then started to sing again, and again, He said, "Feed my sheep." In obedience, I open my mouth and speak to those who can't be in church on Sundays. Love the Lord and be encouraged. Have a nice day....

# Day 61

Good Morning! How can two walk together unless they agree? Read Amos 23. Be careful who you agree with; only agree with the truth. Do not let yourself be persuaded by fools. Have a nice day....

# Day 62

Good Morning! There is a reason why there are meetings. It is to keep the people informed of what is going on in an organization. All levels of businesses meet to get pertinent information out so that it will run properly. When some people aren't able to attend, it is upper management's job to see that the people are informed. Aren't you so glad that God sent out His son to inform us of His ways, so that his church will run according to his plan? You will never have to be concerned about God not meeting with you. He is never to busy, and He is never doing something so important not to see about you, and then tell you, you should have called him first. God loves you so much, that He had a meeting about you before you were born. Remember He said, "Let us make man in our image", Read Genesis 1. He never meant for you to be left out. Be available to meet with your Lord daily to get your instructions so that your part in the organization will run smoothly, so that when you stand before him, He will say well done my  good and faithful servant, Read Matthew 25. Be prudent in the ways of the Lords. And all will be well. Have a nice day....

# Day 63

Good Morning! As you go about your day, think about all the things that God has done for you and your family. There are so many blessings that have been bestowed upon us. These little things should make you smile right about now. Now keep that smile throughout your day. When something rises up to make you want to shake your head.... Just think back to something that God has done for you and pray that He will do the same for that person. Have a nice day....

# Day 64

Good Morning! There is nothing like starting your day with a hot cup of coffee or tea to warm your insides. But better yet the word of God to warm your heart. We all must be reminded that we are not perfect and that no one is, so forgiveness is the key to a washed and cleansed heart, for the heart is desperately wicked and who can know it but the Lord, Read Jeremiah 17. The Lord, and coffee and tea go hand in hand in the mornings. Have a nice day....

# Day 65

Good Morning! When you begin to follow the guidance of the Lord, don't be surprised when challenges arise. How else will you have a chance to prove your spiritual growth? This is where you have to actually make a decision to go against the grain of your selfish thoughts and do the right thing according to what will please God, and then you will reap the benefits of his blessings. It is called pressing through. Have a nice day....

# *Day* 66

Good Morning! Friendship... Are you a good friend to someone? I want to be a good friend to you. I want you to know that this inspiring message is to let you know that God uses me to remind you of just how special you are. If someone is there for you when you are in need, you know you have a friend in deed. A friend will also pray for you even when you haven't seen them. A friendship will last a life time when respect is truly given and received. Have a nice day....

# Day 67

Good Morning! There is the whole truth of a matter: when there is good, there is bad, where there is hot, there is cold; and there is light and there is darkness. We can't have one without knowing the other, search out a matter thoroughly. If someone is only looking at life through rose color glasses and think life will always be rosy, they will be totally disappointed when they take them off. We must see clearly through the eyes of God and all His words. Have a nice day....

# *Day 68*

Good Morning! I want you to look and really see someone around you today, look at their countenance, and see if it is heavy. Take time to ask if there is something wrong, if they share with you, ask if you can pray for them, and be led by the spirit. We are put in someone's path to uplift our Lord and to help others. You will be amazed at how the Lord can and will use you when you're opened up to His will. Have a nice day....

# Day 69

Good Morning! Compassion is an emotion that causes the heart to feel the grace of God move in you for others. When you know of others pain, you don't judge, but come to their aide and support. We pray for others because of this. Please allow the compassion of Christ to move in you that will cause you to look to others needs today, the Lord said, "for what we have done for the least of theses we have done for Him." Read Matthew 25. Have a nice day....

# *Day* 70

Good Morning! For I know the plans that I have for you declares the Lord, plans to prosper you and not to harm you, plans to give you hope and a future. Read Jeremiah 29:11 (NIV). Don't listen or receive the lies of Satan about fear for the future. God did not give you the spirit of fear. Go enjoy your life and day in the Lord. Have a nice day....

# Day 71

Good Morning! Yesterday, I had the privilege of meeting a centenarian. He was in good health and of sound mind and was full of joy. I shared with him about my foster mother, Aunt Ida Mae who is 97; lives alone and is of sound mind, and also full of joy. The Lord said honor thy mother and Father so that you may live long in the land that the Lord your God is giving you. Read Exodus 20. How are you treating your parents, so that you will know how to treat others? Have a nice day....

# $\mathcal{D}ay$ 72

Good Morning! Have you ever had a problem that seems so hard to overcome? Habits are formed by repeated actions that take over from our conscientious; when we try to break them, it seems impossible: smoking, drinking, gossiping, lying, porn, etc. We have to give these things to God, otherwise we only suppress them.... they will rise again when you least expect. The true surrender of these desires can only be set free through Christ, for with Him all things are possible. Read Matthew 19:26. Have a nice day....

# Day 73

Good Morning! As you're off to start your day, know that Christ is with you. Trust Him with all your heart, and lean not to your own understanding in matters that don't make sense. Just know that all things work together for the good that love Him and are called according to his great purpose. He didn't say that we would like all things, but that He would cause them to work for our good, and his glory. Read Proverb 3-5 and Romans 8:28. Have a nice day....

# Day 74

Good Morning! Weigh all your decisions against the word of God today. You may think you know the answer to something, and may try to make things work out the way you want it to go; but if it does not give you peace, then it is something that needs God's wisdom. Trust in the Lord, for all your directions, He will make it clear to you. Wrong decisions will affect the blessings that are at hand (Proverbs 3:5, Read Proverbs 3. Have a nice day....

# Day 75

Good Morning! Lord please help me to live holy before you today. We are sinners save by your holy grace; it is only through your Holy Spirit that we can achieve this. We thank you Lord Jesus for interceding for us in our short-comings. Lord let our lives reflect your love and grace today. Have a nice day....

# Day 76

Good Morning! I experienced the sorrow of parents that lost their child due to drinking and driving. The Lord tells us to mourn with those who mourn and to rejoice with those who rejoice. Friends train your children in the wisdom of God; the fun they seek should not come from something that will lead to death. Be careful how you live before them. Please lead them to Christ that leads to life everlasting life. Have a nice day....

# *Day* 77

Good Morning! What are you putting before your eyes? I turned on the TV and could not believe what I saw and heard: total nudity, even though it was faded over, the things that came out of a female actress mouth was shocking. There is a songstress, and her music videos are nothing but soft porn, and I asked myself, what are we letting our youth watch? The Lord said there will mockery of sin in the last days (Jude 1:18 NIV); well it is here. Parents we must guard what our children see or they will be doing the same things. Have a nice day....

# Day 78

Good Morning! Just be kind to others today, it is not that hard. Satan is cunning. He will sneak into situations and make a mountain out of a mole hill. Don't you let him blow things out of proportion for you today? Allow the spirit of God to rule you in every situation. Let His spirit rule you through His love and understanding, because when we don't, there will be much confusion and who needs that. Have a nice day....

# *Day* 79

Good Morning! How will you write this paragraph of your story today, will it cause someone to smile, and laugh, and to be grateful? Only you can determine the outcome. Remember do unto others as you would have others do unto you, Read Matthew 25. When you love yourself, then God can surely show you how to love others. What you do does not have to be big and bold, just the act of kindness and patience. Have a nice day....

# *Day 80*

Good Morning! Your hope and expectancy is here, rejoice in your baby steps. When you keep plugging away at the goals set before you, and placing your trust in the Lord, all will be well. God knows the plans that He has for you, and no plans of an enemy can stop it, no matter how many arrows have been pulled out of its quiver. If God said it about you before the foundation of this world His will, will be done accordingly. There is only one condition, and that is that we walk with a humble spirit and follow the ways of Christ! Have a nice day....

# *Day 81*

Good Morning! To all that know the Lord, you know you must be faithful to Him for His plans to come true for you. Example: Saul was made king and even died king but was stripped of the anointing of the position, yet also, David was made king and even failed at some major decisions. The difference was David had a repenting heart and delighted his self in the Lord. Will you delight yourself in your Father? Remember pride goes before the fall. Read Psalm 37. Have a nice day....

# Day 82

Good Morning! God is great, God is awesome, God is magnificent, God is a wonder, God is all powerful, God is love, God is all. The only way to get to Him is through Jesus, and the only way to experience Him is by His Holy Spirit. God will not share His honor or glory with anyone, because He is a jealous God. Who are you bowing before? Who are you running after that did not give you life and life everlasting? Stop! Bow before no man because this does not please your most Holy God. I say bow before Him and Him alone. Have a nice day....

# Day 83

Good Morning! I had the pleasure of attending a luncheon for women of distinction, "Our Seasoned Citizens." What these 12 women had in common besides all being over 90 years of age; one lady being 100 years old? And, on no medicine, was they all severed our mighty God. They came to Christ at an early age and never swayed their loyalty to Him. They all showed love to others and all shared Gods wisdom to the youth of their families and their communities. God has honored them with long lives. How are you planning to spend your days? I hope it will be to serve God and others for that is the will of God. Have a nice day....

# *Day 84*

Good Morning! When praises and thankfulness goes up before God, you are preparing to receive the move of His almighty hand. The tribe of Judah went before Israel, (Judah means praise), before entering into any battle, so let us do the same as an example. We must praise our God for what we expect Him to do for us. Remember, I love you, but God and Christ love you more. In the mean time, continue to have a nice day....

# Day 85

Good Morning! Someone once asked me who was my inspiration? My answer was God and Christ. I am also inspired by friends that have lives that are reflective of Christ. We carry the power to influence others, but I want my life, which is: words, actions, and deeds, which do not belong to me, to inspire others to know that there is a God, the King of Kings, and through Him you can do all things. You can love and lead others to a higher purpose for their good and God's glory. Have a nice day....

# Day 86

Good Morning! When you show yourself friendly you will have friends. Relationships? What you put in them is what you will get out of them. Have you showed value to the important people in your lives? Live your lives free with forgiveness of those who have disappointed you, no one is perfect, let alone you. So, just as God and others have forgiven you your trespasses, forgive others. Life is so short, so show love and value to those around you before it's too late. Have a nice day....

# Day 87

Good Morning! Today is the day the Lord has made, let all of us humble ourselves and praise Him for it. Let us give always, and it shall be given back to you. Plant good seeds my friends and reap the harvest of what you sow, remember, if you plant corn you won't get wheat, you will only get back whatever it is you have put out there. So my dear friends watch what you plant. Have a nice day....

# *Day 88*

Good Morning! Charity begins in the heart. Did you know it is better to think of others first than yourself? For what you will find out is, that by taking care of others, someone else will take care of you. When charity comes from your heart, God is touched. When you give because someone shames you into giving, you may as well keep it, because the motive is forced and not of love. Remember what you do and give for God out of a pure heart will last forever. Have a nice day....

# Day 89

Good Morning! The beautiful thing about the innocence of children is that they believe all that we tell them. They look at us with receiving eyes and eager souls to please us. When we tell them fairy tales, they have such smile upon their faces, and always enjoy hearing; "… and they lived happily ever after." Well, it is good for us to be childlike before the Lord, to believe all that He tells us, and we will truly live a life to be happy ever after, for real. Let us all live to believe Him for He is not a man that He should lie. Have a nice day....

# *Day 90*

Good Morning! Sometimes we have to stand still and see the move of God's hand in a situation that is bigger than us. Keep on doing well, keep your faith, and trust your Father. God is a God of justice, you may have to wait quite a while to see his results, but remember all things will work out for your good and His glory. Have a nice day....

# Day 91

Good Morning! I think it is so nice when someone takes their time to pay us a compliment, but, I think it is even kinder to pay a compliment back. Isn't it nice to hear kind things about ourselves? Yes it is, so besides just sayings thank you, also say something kind back to the giver of their kind thoughts, then all of us will smile. Have a nice day....

# Day 92

Good Morning! Me and many of my friends have been experiencing difficult situations lately; arrows flying at us. There is a blessing coming our way. We are being stretched; made to deal with things and emotions that will prepare us for our next season. How can we stand in our new promotion without knowing how to handle unexpected trials and tribulations correctly? He, God, who is sending us, will also prepare us. He said, to rejoice when persecutions comes your way. For we know, He is in this with us; so we STAND. Have a nice day....

# Day 93

Good Morning! The thoughts you entertain in your heart will bring forth actions you make. What will be the thoughts that will bring forth positive actions for yourself and others today? Have a nice day....

# Day 94

Good Morning! How is grace evident in your life? Grace is shown by the kindness that you show to others, overlooking their small faults. It is the polished behavior that comes with maturity from applying Gods divine practices. God's grace is on us daily because of His love towards us. Will you be willing to share God's grace to others today even when it feels hard to do? Have a nice day....

# Day 95

Good Morning! This can be a new beginning for you today. Did you ever watch the show, what would you do? For us to be salt and light, that means that you have to make a decision to do or say the right thing in a bad situation... Are you willing? I heard some ladies speaking ill of another, as I listened, I noticed that the thing that they were speaking of, one of them was guilty of that same thing, so, as the light in the situation, I went to the one and whispered in her ear the thing that she needs to fix for herself. That ended the conversation about the other person that they were talking ill against. Salt changes the flavor of things. Have a nice day....

# *Day 96*

Good Morning! I would hope as you get ready for your day, that you would make time to spend in God's word. Visit with Jesus, so that He can fill up your cup, so that it will be overflowing. You will be replenished so that you can share with others. We all have to be fed, and refilled, and who else can do the job except someone who is filled and have something to share themselves. Have a nice day....

# Day 97

Good Morning! How does your future look? It will look amazing and bright if you are looking at your life through the eyes of God. He has such great plans, for us, His children, so let us follow him to the end. Life will have its test, but they are only designed to prepare us for the future that He had planned for us from the beginning. Have a nice day....

# *Day 98*

Good Morning! Choices... When God gives you a window of opportunity for growth and development for yourself with others, how will you choose? Will you only think of yourself and miss that door that will leads to your blessing, or will you recognize what God is doing right then and right now, some doors only open once. Have a nice day....

# Day 99

Good Morning! Live your life with an open heart for others, keep patience in mind when you speak and act, and all will be well. Accept gifts with gratitude, so that when you share with others the law of giving will continue to grow. Do not give with the expectancy of getting something back in return; give because you want to see the seed of giving grow. Have a nice day....

# Day 100

Good Morning! Who are you putting first in your life? The Lord said He will have no other Gods before him. The family comes next, fathers and mothers. The Lords said to honor your mother and father that your days may be long on this earth, (He never gives you an excuse no matter what, not to keep this command). Families are under the first attack of Satan from the beginning of time. The husbands are to honor their wives, and wives are to respect their husbands. Families under God's rules will make it, even when they come under opposition; this is the only way to raise honorable children for His kingdom. Have a nice day....

# Day 101

Good Morning! Stay in tune with your spirit and listen to what you have fed it, there are so many other voices to draw you astray. Sometimes there will be third party voices, he said, she said, this and that, don't bother to chase and to prove, be still in the confidence of who you are, and the Christ in you. You have come too far to be distracted now. We must all stay on our guard against the wiles of the enemy. Have a nice day....

# Day 102

Good Morning! May the thoughts of having a nice day, and someone thinking of you, warms your heart as a hot cup of coffee or tea warms your soul. Remember, I love you but God and Christ loves you more. Have a nice day....

# Day 103

Good Morning! The name above all names, and the things that may come against you, call on the name of Jesus. He is your rock and your hope; for all that you stand in need of. Remember that is what He died for. You are never alone! Have a nice day....

# Day 104

Good Morning! Did you ever look at something that has happened in your life and see the impossible that has occurred? Right now, I am so thankful for the hand of God upon me and you. He keeps us from dangers, known and unknown. Raise your hand to Him right now and thank Him for keeping you safe on the highways and byways. I am sending up prayers for all the drivers of the world today. Please stand with me. Have a nice day....

# Day 105

Good Morning! Ask the Lord of Lords to create a new heart in you today as David did; only God knows the heart of a man and He said that it is full of deceit, and who can know it, Read Revelation 12. Satan will use your past to keep you hostage, for Satan is the accuser of the brethren and the reminder of your past, which can't be changed. When you spend time with the Lord you will find wisdom of the freedom in Christ by His forgiveness, and the renewing of your mind so that you can be a blessing to others and not a hindrance. Have a nice day....

# Day 106

Good Morning! Who is standing by you, and who are you standing with? We are not meant to be alone; in God wonderful creation, we are meant to enjoy it and others. Let's keep our eyes open so that we do not miss the beauty of all that He gave us, in spite of all the things we have to deal with daily. Let us look up towards heaven and be thankful. Have a nice day....

# Day 107

Good Morning! I want to say simply what the Lord has said this morning. How can you say that you love God who you have not seen, and not love the man right next to you that you do see? Read 1 John 4. Remember, God is love and to not love everyone is a sin. We are to love everyone because He first loved us, while we were still yet sinners, this is not a choice but a commandment, and we can't do this in our own strength, but through the power of God's Holy Spirit. Are you filled with His spirit of love?, if not, ask Him to fill you with his agape love. Have a nice day....

# Day 108

Good Morning! What will your dream cost you? There is a price to pay for everything that you invest in. Sometimes you will lose the most valuable things that God has given you, if you make the wrong investments with your thoughts and time; on the other hand, since Christ died for you, you can have all that He said you can have if you invest in His holy plans. You can have peace in times of trouble, which we all have, security when times are uncertain, and love everlasting from the ones that matter most. Have a nice day....

# Day 109

Good Morning! Thinking of others will keep you humble, and confidence in yourself will make you bold. The Lord tells us to come boldly before His throne, and how can you do that without a broken and contrite spirit? We cannot come to God just any way we want, but the only way He said we can, humbly, humble doesn't mean weak, it means knowing your strength and power and authority and surrendering it to God to be used for others. Will you pray with me for all the sick and homeless today? Have a nice day....

# Day 110

Good Morning! Did you know that when the Lord said that He will bless the works of your hands that He means that the gifts in you will be a blessing for others? There is nothing that the Lord gives us that is just for ourselves, it is not to gain all the wealth of the world and then lose your soul. But, that He may use you to open doors for others; that even more souls will be blessed. Have a nice day....

# Day 111

Good Morning! What door will you walk through today? We are given a choice each morning of how we want our day to go. We can choose to put everything before our Lord and Father God, or we can choose to plunge into our day head on carrying things in our own strength and thinking. I hope that you would choose to let God direct your steps; it will make for a much more pleasant day. Have a nice day....

# *Day 112*

Good Morning! When we have asked forgiveness of the Lord of a matter, and we mean it in our hearts, true repentance means to turn from that sin and to go in another direction, God's direction. God has forgiven you, now you must forgive yourself, do not listen to the lies of the enemy of your soul when He tries to remind you of things you once did. We are to walk in the total newness of our freedom in Christ. Have a nice day....

# Day 113

Good Morning! God wants you to know that everything that He has for you will be yours, and no devil in hell can stop His plan, when you make the right choices in Him. Pray for those that will come against His plans, because vengeance is mine saith the Lord, Read Roman 12. Encouragement comes with the knowledge that there may be some difficult days, but all will be well in the Lord. Have a nice day....

# Day 114

Good Morning! When we look into faces of others today, and someones head is hung a little low, or their smile isn't that bright, let us remember to say, "all is well", and let us send a warm smile their way. They could be under the burden of bad news in their families, or other things that are weighing their hearts down. Let's let them see the Christ in us, to be reminded of the Christ in them, because all will really be well with Him in control. Have a nice day....

# Day 115

Good Morning! The wonderful thing about childbirth is that you get to hold, care and cherish a new born baby. That child comes to depend upon you for everything. When you are carrying your baby in your arms, they are so secure that they are safe, they have no fear at all of falling, this is a bond that will last a life time. Well, that is the same bond we have with God the Father, He will never let us fall, but if we do slip, He is right there to pick us up again and set us back on our way. Have a nice day....

# Day 116

Good Morning! The spirit of wisdom shall lead you into all understanding. The plots of your enemies shall fall every time when you are guided by the Holy Spirit. The plot of the enemy of your soul is to kill, steal, and destroy you. The Lord said, Read Matthew 10, be as wise as a serpent and as gentle as a dove, the victory is already yours, don't be drawn into a battle without the full armor of the Lord which was given to you through Jesus Christ our Lord. Have a nice day....

# Day 117

Good Morning! You must learn to encourage yourself today. When the enemy comes in like a flood, you must hold on to the standards raised by Christ. We are all called to battle, but how can we take the victory that belongs to us if we don't know how to use our sword. Stay in the word of God and surround yourself with wise Godly counsel, and all will be well. Have a nice day....

# Day 118

Good Morning! God will make a way out of no way when we seek his advice. Temptations will arise in our lives, but not before God have already made a way for you to escape. Remember when the door opens that leads to destruction, Holy Spirit is there to say, child come this way, don't go that way, and therefore; you will come out triumphantly, and with more wisdom to boot. Have a nice day....

# Day 119

Good Morning! This is a day where you can do something so sufficient, and yet very simple, it is called standing for the truth. Don't let yourself be drawn into co-signing someone else's version of what's not true just to fit in. The truth will always be revealed. Sometimes later than we wish, but this gives you time to make the right decisions right now. You can be sure that your sins will find you out. I want you to stand strong in the Lord and the power of His might for He is truth. Have a nice day....

# *Day* 120

Good Morning! No matter what comes your way today, you are fully equipped to handle it. The power of Christ will sustain you. We must be slow to speak unhealthy words, and we must stand on what we know to be the truth of Christ, and not facts that we see. The Lord said the truth will set you free, and also, whose report are you going to believe, Read John 8. So, if things get a little hectic today, be settled, by knowing you are not in this thing alone. Have a nice day....

# Day 121

Good Morning! Do you know why it is good to confess? This allows us to be free from what binds our hearts and minds. I confess that I am a sinner saved by grace through faith in Jesus Christ, Read Roman 10. Secrets will keep you sick, wondering when something is going to be found out or uncovered. The Lord said what is done in the dark will eventually come to light, Read Mark 4. I confess that I am nothing, and can do nothing, without Christ, and that I need Him and His words to cleanse my heart and my ways each and every day. Have a nice day....

# Day 122

Good Morning! The cost of friendship is your time. You may not always have time to visit them because of all the things we are involved in, but when we do take the time to make that phone call, or e-mail that friend or family member, we are saying that you are important to me and that I am thinking of you. It is sometimes the smallest things we do that will make others smile, and we will smile too. Have a nice day....

# Day 123

Good Morning! The comfort we take today is in the knowledge of Gods words. His wisdom is infinite and His word is final. His thoughts are higher than ours and His ways are not at all like ours. Let us remember to seek Him with all our hearts, and Christ will renew our minds with the power of the Holy Spirit. All is well through our Lord, for He gave us his word for every situation, because there is nothing new under the sun. Have a nice day....

# *Day 124*

Good Morning! I want you to know that by the grace of God, I send you encouragements, to embolden, and edify you each day, because without God, Christ,and the Holy Spirit this is just another new age message, which it is not. The most important message that I want to share with you is that without the blood of Jesus, we just exist. Choose this day who you will serve, as for me and my house, we will serve the Lord (Joshua 24:15). Have a nice day....

Made in the
USA
Lexington, KY